CW00670402

SCARS AND SUTURES

Scars and Sutures

KHRYS KANE

KhrysKane

Contents

Copyright © 2024 by Khrys Kane

All rights reserved. No part of this book may be reproduced in
any manner whatsoever without written permission except in
the case of brief quotations embodied in critical articles and
reviews.

First Printing, 2024

To the Creon, Thrasymachus & Vilgefortz types:

For if people are going to blast holes in me with either their malice or "misunderstandings", I might as well be compensated for the trust and ammunition I naively provide.

Calling Honesty

Honesty is the cornerstone of intimacy, authenticity
Honesty not only with others
But honesty with ourselves
May we find the freedom in a sacred space
To consort with our shadow self, unfettered
Without deceit or delusion
And resolve to guard the freedom of others
To do the same

My Demons Aren't Buried

I don't bury my demons;
I heal them and
put them on staff.

Message in
a Bottle

I bled into a bottle
Sent the message on its way
Some days went by
Before I sent another

I waited
And I waited
And I waited

> Botched a cut
> Made a mess
> Wrote an apology note
> With my own red paint
> And my finger strokes

I waited
And I waited
And I waited

Again I bled
Into a bottle
Sent the message
On its way

I waited
And I waited
And I waited

How many heartbeats have I bled
In my quest to be understood?

Still I bleed into bottles
Still I write in my own blood
Still I wait

Modus Operandi

I used to leave things
Slowly
Painfully
With fervent protests
Then
Suddenly
Quietly
All at once

Water Roots

Past first bloom
Wilted and waning
No seedling, my perennial heart
Uprooted, isolated, immersed
Growing roots in the spring of life

Something Delphic This Way Comes

I am usually quite skilled at identiftying
How I am or will be misunderstood
A language teacher
Knows the mistakes
Common to a student
The difference between affect and effect
Which French vowels, overpronounced
Connotations different between dead and murdered

I am usually quite skilled at identifying
How I am or will be misunderstood
Nevertheless, I am surprised
Occasionally, by a new way of being misunderstood
Often, by the fact that I was misunderstood
Always, by my own surprise

Dragon-Rider: Part 2

This dragon I straddle
kept bringing me back
to wreckage
I would have rather moved on from
as if it knows something
I don't

Love at First Sight

I believe in love at first sight
Not because at nineteen I fancied myself in love
With a man I had barely spoken to
Although it was then that I learned
Weak at the knees was not just a metaphor
Knees soon baked crimson
By the summer sun

No, it was not love
Although my youth so dreamed
I did not know I was an addict then
Raw ingredients of longing, idealized fascination
So perfectly soluable with absence, unmet needs
I was the mixologist, shaking with hope
Gurlging the only cocktail I could make
The only thing I knew then of love was its ache

She had me by her spirit
Grabbing the edge of her travel cage
Like Mufasa gripping the precipice of that cliff

Mewling in protest at the mage hand
Relocating her to another confinement
I watched her with her siblings, caught in a thrall
Her tiny little white boots, bright green eyes
I held her tiger stripes against my heart
And she was home
My love at first sight

My Place, My Space

When I say I need my space
That's why I have my own place
I don't just mean I self-soothe with aesthetic:
my home is the nucleus of that mechanism
I also mean: I need a space
where I am not beholden to anyone else
a place where I do not owe an explanation
for my presence
a space where the only expectations
on the guest list are mine
a place to go where I owe gratitude
only to myself

Wounds Never Seen

Your hands taught me
A touch
Does not have to be
Angry
To be
Cruel

Haunted

My body is a haunted house
that I carry with me
Wisps of unfinished business
Wander my halls
Some floorboards creak
Under new weight
Whole rooms have been abandoned
With the figment of closure
Locked in statis
A time capsule
Of another life

"Not Me"

Our house was haunted
Growing up
The one ghost we named
Amongst the many we didn't
We called "Not Me"

It was not known for much
(at the time)
Dishes in the sink
Leaving our lights on
After we had all left the room

A puckish spirit maybe then
Might have taken the blame
For breaking the face of Hercules
Plate, shattered on a wall
Had I not seen my father
Yeet it from his own hand

Foreshadowing

Once in a dream
I was shot in the throat
Outside my grandparents' home
By a guy on a skateboard
An apt metaphor
For every time I've died a little
Murdered in a place I should have been safe
By someone I didn't expect

Shadow Vision

Don't underestimate my willingness
to crawl around
in my own darkness.
I've lived in the shadow of others' demons
for so long
I no longer fear my own.

Changing
the Menu

Don't, don't ask about it
you'll offend the chef
    barrages of protests bounce, frenetic:
    you must think that I'm terrible
    you are nitpicky, critical
    nothing is ever good enough for you
    you are so selfish
    you only care about yourself
  don't you have any empathy
      the effort that I've put into this endeavor
      what I need to run this place

you sit there, a hostage
to the captor who feeds you
the anomalies in the patterns
spearing the only source of stability
they don't care, you didn't pick 'em
you're here under extreme duress

it's not your fault you require the
fundamentals of humanity
they knew those evolutionary needs
before they trapped you,
biting off more than they could chew
you say: either boundaries are on the menu
or my next meal is you

The Foot Races of
Morpheus
and Eros

The embrace of sleep and love
Are much the same
Not for the quiet comfort
Their restoration
Or the frequency of a dream
But for that the more you chase
The more they elude

Interdisciplinary Studies

Generals and anthropologists
study humanity differently
But a child born in chaos
Is something of both

Aphrodite's Addict

I have never craved a drink
The way I ached for love
The guilt of a night overdone
Never consumed me or
Plumbed me to depths
The likes of which
Has my affection
I was but a fly in the trap
of Aphrodite's embrace.
My love, a dove, sacrificed
Wilted feathers, inking pomegranate

Cautiously Cryptic

When did you learn to hide in the nuance,
where the shadows of their assumptions shade you?
When my call became a cry without meaning;
sometime after that, I answered.

Mirror Man

Did you see me?
Or through my vulnerability with you
Did I begin to see myself?
I fell in love with my own heart
Baring it for you

I gave you a piece of myself, more than flesh
That is the deepest cut
The one that still aches
I spill my heart out on these pages
And you are no longer special

Devils Dancing in
the Dark

I don't think you're the devil
Not that you've ever asked me
Always too busy trying to tell me
What I think

Seeing the devil in you
Is not to see you as a devil
Many heartbreaks I might have avoided
If that were true

Well acquainted with my own shadow
I was just as ready to love you in your own
If you had just been honest
With the both of us

My forgiveness is real
But not enough to buy my silence
That tacit compliance

The only thing you truly desired

If reincarnation is real
If our souls are recylcing and re-recycling
Until they've been purged of our junk
Purified by our adversity
If we only get to rest in the oblivion that bore us
When this is done
I think you have more lives left to live

You are the kind of lifelong criminal
That never gets confined
What the devil has in concentration
You make up for in longevity

For all my honesty and vulnerability
You are better at weaponizing your fragility
Than I've ever been
My mother would like you
Although she could teach you a thing or two
About delivering a backhanded compliment

When you said you didn't want me
To think you had it all together
I kept the kind of quiet the grown get
When a child looks for woods in the wardrobe

What a rare species of reassurance
There was never any risk

I would have sooner been lit aflame
By the autumn rain

I speak now
Unequivocably
The way you should have

Bitch

You're right
I am a bitch
I took a nip at your heel
Instead of curling up
With docile affection
At your feet
To wag in gratitude
At the table scraps
You'd feed me

Honestly

Voices in my head
A cacophony I can't quite quiet

They speak of sabotage
They say we came with a warning label, a disclaimer
We communicated honestly, too honestly, they say
Heart on our sleeve, honest
"Off our meds", honest
Bids for connection, honest
Lack of connection makes us honest
Reactionary even, honestly

They cut me off from lines of support
Lines of communication
Lines of honest
Then blamed me for my honesty
And my own misery, honestly

Carnival Cowards

Cowards flee their own likeness
They'll say they're in a fun house:
That they're seeing a distortion of their true selves
You need to be defective, darling
They're dishonest too on their own
But they prefer their reflection when they're alone

They'll thank you for your vulnerability
Mistrust you on the same account
Give you a little grace
Just to throw it in your face
Woo you when you're cautious
Lead you on when you're reserved
Ask you to remove the mask
Bitch out when the same you ask

Not Your Puzzle

Did you think I was a puzzle?
By that I am not asking
Whether you thought I was:
Complicated
Time-consuming
Multi-faceted
Fun
Challenging
Or worthy of your mantle

I mean: is it even remotely possible
you thought that I have a finite number
of static characteristics
that you could have knowledge of them all
possess them
be able to perceive them, piece them
in exactly the correct way?

Distractions

A welcome interruption to thoughts
I wish I could pack away
Shove in a closet corner
Until enough time has passed
That they hold no meaning for me anymore
Then they can be buried
In earnest
With no hope of resurrection

Four Letter Words

Little men on a map
A game of conquest
Turned a loving face
Blue with spittle
My retreat into a corner
Trailed by the shadow
Of my father's exasperation
He rolled his eyes
"That man loves you"

The Reoccuring Daydream

I would run away from home
There was always woods nearby
Mountains not too far off course
I would be found by a handsome man
Who lived in a cave
A couple clicks from a river
This river eventually led back to my past life
I never ventured too close to it alone
In this cave this man would care for me
For reasons I never even imagined

I am not the type to welcome pity
Yet I have never associated a sense of justice
A recognition of wrong doing
Or a desire to rectify a wrong and heal a wound
With pity
So perhaps I am the type to welcome pity
If that is how you define it

And I simply did not contemplate that anyone noble
In my dream, he is always noble
Would need a reason besides

No Contact

They say there is no sound in space
I guess that's where the words went
After their gasp
Now, for me, you
Echo into nothingness

Memorial For the Lost

That midnight in the Big Easy
Solemn memorial, in a city of many
One stands for the lost, the unclaimed
I realized something then:
why I used to want to mean something
to someone
even if it killed me
I fear neither dying
nor even dying alone
I am afraid of no one noticing
when I am gone
it would only validate
my birth as a mistake
the one of my Demons
I still fear

Home

I told him once he felt like home
What I thought I meant was
Home: the home I always wanted
What I actually said was
Home: the home I had
The difference was cavernous
But I was not yet healed enough
To know when I switched dialects
Without meaning to

There and Not There

Your husband was surprised
When I came to celebrate your life
And I know I dissociated through your dying
All the bedside prayers
I was there and not there
But when you were here
When you were you
When your heartbeat was more
Than a hospital sound machine
I was there
Eleventh hour notice
I was there
Trying to build a life
While you fighting for yours
I was there
I was there
I was there

But when I drew a line in the sand
I guess the die was cast
I didn't know it had to be all
Or nothing
I don't know why
It had to be all or nothing

She asked me if I could pick her up from the airport
You know, that was the first thing she said to me
My head started wheeling, reminding her
Which daughter she called
She just said, "I know" then
Repeated her question

I asked, "When?"
That's how I found out
You were dying already
In the state and city I lived in
For real this time

The Compost Bin

Scrappings of something healthy
I once had, now putrid
Fodder for future growth

Bare
Minimum Shit

The truth is you only liked me
When I didn't expect anything from you
You liked me when every little thing you did
Was above and beyond, a real treat
Using me to feed your savior complex
Milking my affections and admiration for your ego
You only ever wanted to give me
That bare minimum shit

You promised me the world
A support system
Intentional community
People I could count on
The only dream I would have given anything for
Got me invested, attached
Then found a reason, any reason
All the reasons possible
To switch it up

The goalposts moved
Mine, yours, doesn't matter
As long as you decided, controlled
Whose and when and how and where
You only wanted to give me
That bare minimum shit

This ending was written
Long before I read the ink
With the chance to do it over
Our tragedy would only have more text
This was not a choose your own adventure
You meticulously curated a fantasy
Had me blindfolded
Sticking pins in myself
You only wanted to give me
That bare minimum shit

Now it's all too much
I am too much
I expect too much
You claim you lack the intent for malice
But you lacked it for community
And honest communication too
Which still makes you a damn hypocrite and liar
The truth is you only liked me
When I liked you on your terms
You liked me when it was it was convenient
And you liked me when that was all okay with me

You only ever wanted to give me
That bare minimum shit

Once you had me on the hook
Just enough tension on the line
Where you could reel me in
If and when
When and if
That's where you wanted me to stay
Baited on your hook
Stuck on your line
Getting reeled in on that bare minimum shit

The Discard

I let you treat me like a joint
You hit when you needed a puff
Of dopamine
When my tolerance for it burnt out
I wondered why you
Dropped me

This Is Not A Real Apology, I Know

Spent a full moon cycle
On the other side of the pond
Years ago

Last night I was thinking, remembering
How they don't stipulate every term
They would expect their interactions
To defy the specific bounds of their writing
The principles are illustrative
Contracts are guidelines
For a relationship
No one presumes the writing is complete
Exhaustive
But we are American are we not?

I'm sorry I didn't know
I needed the terms of our friendship
In writing

I'm sorry I didn't know
If it wasn't in our most recent, whatever it was we had
It didn't exist

I'm sorry I didn't know
What you said came with an implied
Merger clause
I'm sorry I didn't recognize
Illusory promises when I saw them

Except maybe I did:
I lashed out before I knew
Like really really knew
I felt it first, our heart stop
Tried to jolt us back to beating
Learned the hard way
You already gained the benefit
Did not want us revived
I'm sorry I tried

Tickling Poseidon

Wagging my tongue
I was as Xerxes
Whipping the sea

Dotted Lines

the day starts under stars
drumming on pavement, paced by the heart
giving chase, pack in formation
when the intrusion of daylight finds us
intercepted by a delegation
interrupted by a delineation
We signed up for this

our daylight is decimated by indecision
an astral projection always in every avenue
coherence, defenestrated
we race towards patience
delirious with the distortions disguising
might makes right in a subterfuge
We signed up for this

the clock ticks lengths with each recounting
speaking of betrayals in gardens
without a friend to give an ear
patriarchy breaching gates by force and false horses

crowning women with snakes and
recounting sympathies for a nursery of hearts of stone
They didn't sign up for this

our enemies shelter under the shields
of battle buddies flipped
the clash of clemency whittling at our world
what is it about charisma that drugs the masses
tells them the only way to survive
is to inject corruption in their veins
We didn't sign up for this

no longer do I care to wear the perfume of duty
the odor assails my nostrils
my mouth floods with copper
I am a handful of sand sprinkled over the visage
of an unburied corpse; see what I've suffered
for the love of the world I live in
I didn't sign up for this

Tell-Tale Treasure

"Bury it," you said
my Evil Eye saw depressions in chests
cardio couldn't fix
my lips refused to dance to harmonies off pitch
this haunting heart still beat while breaking

"Bury it," you said
you meant bury it like a body,
but I buried it like treasure
now the cadence beats from nightstand tables
thrums from bookstore shelves

Objection: Relevance

A realization, far belated
seeded by comments
from plural sources
of ambiguous relevance
An epiphany, far behind
years of furrowed brows

You might have thought
It would actually explain a lot
You might have thought that I colored my criticism
with your Blackness.

I healed more
Forgave some
When I thought I better understood
Your reprisals

Healing Isn't Linear

I know I'm still healing
I know that's okay
But I'm ready for the day
With a little less feeling
With a little less reeling

In the Line
of Duty

I think you might have saved my life
Long after you took your own

    Special victims' counsel
      Isolated
        No support system
          Hibernating all weekend
        Workplace tensions
      Insomnia
    Vicarious trauma

Behavioral Health barely blinked
    Say "family history"
      All of a sudden
        What?
      I wasn't just "being dramatic?"
    I don't know
I guess nobody wanted the paperwork

Ostracism

There were a few times I knew my name
would be etched into the ostracon
I contradicted out loud
what was meant to be
suggested and understood
the veracity, the accuracy of text
matters not
when the subtext is meant
to carry the weight of
Authority

I underestimated for not quite the last time
the rally point at the status quo
I can almost hear the clink
of all my names
falling like rain
in the election I won
by a landslide

Just a Dream

I thought I had let him go
But one night I dreamt of him
again
He still felt like the home
I always wanted
and never had

With eyes alight, I recalled
the day he called me family
the day I woke up
He wasn't any different
It was a dream
Nothing more

Bury Me with the Broken Broom

one piece of cheap hollow plastic
in each hand
arms crossed in repose
with the symbols of our friendship
Here lies a body turned stale
sweeping her mess of a mind
out with the dust

Blood on the
Tracks

Though I grieve
for the blood
of the abandoned flesh
on the tracks
A part of me envies those
who can stomach only
a concern for themselves
Is my rage more towards them
or towards myself
How many times
must I die
on the tracks
Because I couldn't leave
well enough alone

My Favorite Pair
of Heels

He was my favorite pair of heels
He made feel grand, statuesque
At a time when all I wanted to do
Was hide under the covers
He felt like an adventure
Like going on the town
Like all eyes are on me
But in a fun way:
The never having to pay for your own drinks
Oh my god *look at those shoes* kind of way

After a few turns 'round the clock
I felt like a clown
Can't walk straight, everything hurts
People looking at me now like:
Oh my god why can't she walk in those shoes?
Why'd she even wear them?
Ankle's half sprained—

Totally my fault, right?
I put on the shoes to begin with
Then the heel breaks off,
I'm out there rednecking it with duct tape
I'm too proud to call an Uber

It's after I end up in urgent care, after the X-ray
After the doctors look at me with side eye
Like you're a *smart girl:* What are you doing?
Don't I realize maybe my heels are a problem?
How they used to make me feel
Is a fond memory now, not a reality
The reality is this.
So I put the heels in the closet
Thinking maybe one day I'll fix them
One day I'll get to wear them again

My ankle healed though
And even the memory of my favorite heels
Being my favorite heels
Wasn't enough to make me put them on again

Missing the Mind Twists

A part of me may miss the game, the mind twists
the chemistry of the sexual titillation
I don't miss you

Epiphany

spent all this time
surviving
for other people
waiting for someone
to treat me
like I belong somewhere

when the where and why
of belonging
has been inside me
the whole time

Flight Plan

Did you know then
You wouldn't see them again
A pair of new lives shucked
Over oysters in New Orleans

When the plane touched down
On higher ground
A path began to unfold
Did you yet start to see

When the lights came on at last
Never have you run so fast

Weather Witch
Polyamory

To Winter, I say
give me your darkness, let us enjoy the comfort
of Companionship in the bitter cold
when the nights are long may you have
the grit to withstand the reflections of your own spirit
and Fortitude still to remain amongst mine
Resolute as an unforgiving freeze
Balanced as the first snow
flickering under the phase of the newest moon

To Spring, I say
I welcome your new glow with an open heart
your breeze is sweet and our smiles bloom
when the rains come, the skies cry
of Hope and Rejuvenation
although we know this floral Abundance will pass
the colors here are brightly variegated
and the Joy is pure

To Summer, I say
embrace me in your gaze
but do not begrudge me the shade
although sometimes my skin inflames
like the crackle of fireworks in the sky
there is something here that looks like Freedom
feels like the Ease of a weekend bbq among Comrades
your Warmth has come around enough that
somehow, I Trust that it will come again

To Fall, I say
oscillate as you wish between bright and dreary
I take not your warmth for granted
nor fear a sudden chill
come for me and be mine in time and season
the Splendor of your appearance
and Comfort of your caress
are not mine to experience without interruption
if Inspiration struck with every Dream
I would never rest

When He
Covers You

When he covers you
Does he cover you like soil on a seed
Or a corpse in a coffin

Damaged
Isn't Dead

It was audacity
You thought I only knelt
Because I could not stand

I know which cards
You have in your hand

I dealt them
From my own deck

Did you think
That an accident?

Duality of Chaos

Although I am out of those circles now
And I still can't speak for them
I think any commander would tell you
That a projected loss from an assumed risk
Still fucking hurts sometimes
It's the nature of things
To want things to work out better
To plan for an Order of loss
And have Chaos yet hold our hand
Call it what you want
A gambler's hope
A romantic trope
A hail mary cope
But don't call it naive
If chaos can grip a sword
It can hold a suture

Heartbeats of Desire

I've decided
the only thing I want
is Everything
people don't think I
deserve

Roles of
Retribution

The director screamed in my face
For forgetting lines he never gave me
So I carved out his larynx
And on it played a pretty ditty

The rest of the cast who got their lines
Burdened by the freedom to write their part
Burned me at the stake
And made a meal of my heart

Hidden Galaxies

galaxies are hidden past
within the vast darkness
if it could
would the galaxy
shrink to a star
fall to Earth's brink
with the hope we all
might concieve its existance
percieve it in part
a fraction of its beauty
a trifle of its mystery
a fragment of its intricacy

Monsters Like Me

You tied me up in chains
Traded our affection for my pain
I made a bargain with the monster you left me to feed
May he have me for dessert
But make a meal of you first

Triangulated

Past the threshold
The apex of two staircases
The definition of invited
Cornered
And contained

The Five Stages of Grief

My denial was
telling myself no matter what happened
we'd still be friends
not being able to admit: I knew you were using me
and I was letting you

My bargaining was
afraid of my own boundaries
letting you make me the bad guy
giving you more time
still not bluffing

My anger was
neither unprovoked nor unwarranted
but nevertheless unnecessary
a gift of conflicted connection
you did not deserve

My depression was
gaining another twenty pounds
sleeping the daylight away
a death date set
if I could not exorcise this demon

My acceptance was
not giving you an indefinite amount of time
starting therapy, again
an apartment full of moving boxes and
honest writing

Three Things That Remind Me of You

1. A layer of fresh snow over a coat of ice.
2. A paper airplane in the wind.
3. Driving through a dense Fresno fog

Rules of the Game

The confusion was of your own creation
carved from all your misrepresenatations
As in the stories of the preachers
you were crafting the antidote
for the poisons of your invention
Holding yourself out like a teacher
a facade of aid and instruction
coaxing me to play a proxy
calling it a lesson, me a pupil

Isn't it funny
I only understand the rules of the game
If you have my compliance
Any deviation, independent
You insist I splay myself open
Sure I've misunderstood the rules
You must explain the game, again

Even Lions Bleed

Maybe no one came to save you
Because the state of vulnerability
Does not equate to fragility
A predator can discern the difference
Between wounded lion and injured gazelle
A gazelle will likewise take you for a lion
Even when you are broken and bleeding

Can't Get It Right

I made a batch of porridge, tried to get it right
Too much milk, then not enough
The texture was too light, the grains were too rough
It was too sweet, out of season fruit
Added the wrong meat, didn't use a vegetable root
Tried my hand whittling a chair
To see how I would fare
It was too small for someone so tall
Yet too grand for a Spartan hall
Too rigid for nursery rocking
Excessive plush for office docking
Though I was vexed, the bed I tried next
Less is more, basically an elevated floor
Frilled the bed with thread to ease the chill
Popped on a billow of pillows, gave it a flop
No matter what I did, I couldn't find the pea
The whole thing was an exercise in futility

Not Your
Falling Star

You wanted me at my star,
but not at my galaxy.

Fire Damage

I am not immune
To the threat of these flames
Some resistance there must be
Built in, under this skin
I can hold the heat of anger
Outmatching most
But I am not immune

the mistake I make
is venting what I hold
on friends

My reoccuring delusion:
my attachment is a vaccine
I find myself entangled by the truth
Their trust is the innoculation
I never know
until much too late
they don't have

A Letter from the Imprisoned

The real torture of all this
How little anything I do matters
If my captors wish to harm me
They will find a slight to punish
Percieved perhaps, it matters not
They want me to believe of course
That compliance will serve me too
But the relief is so very fleeting
And when I am alone in the night
I are haunted by the wonder if
I have consented to my own chains

A Letter from the Disillusioned Dreamer

The incredible iconic irony of all this
My torment has become a tourniquet:
Nothing I do matters
Whether in my screaming or my silence
Those who had wished to hear me, heard
Whether vibrant or veiled
Those who had wished to see me, saw
What method by which to measure
How much and yet still how little
Anything has changed
Some captors make competent charlatans
Some captives wander concealed cages
Convinced their confines are chosen
It's all the same game in different frames
I left the table for the fable
And found: nothing I do matters

Not the God of Augustine

I refuse to be a simple creature
I will be complicated, contradictory
I will bathe you in the waters
of my mercy or my vengeance
I could be your hero, I could be your villain
What if I'm neither, what if I'm both
Either way I can promise you this:
I will feign no sorrow, nor remorse
For that which I am unwilling to fix

Sometimes

Sometimes I change the way I speak
Like I shift the way that I hold my pen

Sometimes I look at old scribbles
And honor the past lives
That brought me here

Sometimes I read my own life
Like a novel
Hyperfixating on this character
Or that one

Sometimes finding myself
Feels more like remembering
For in everything I have lost
I have found a piece of myself

The Body I
Survived In

I am much bigger now
An old photo of myself
when i was at my most fit
had me the other day
smiling

I fought for that body then
But I fought for my life
in the body I am in
beauty standards be damned
my body will heal as I do
I don't love my weight
But I refuse to hate
the body I survived in

I Straddle Worlds

The present is a past life
Still being crafted
I sit in the threshold
Between this life and the next
Thus I began to live in earnest
When I no longer cared to

Inking Over You

Penciling me into your life,
a great eraser in the other hand.
If you wanted a clearer say
in the writing of our ending,
you should have grasped a pen.
Too much ink has spilled,
you can no longer scratch your lies
into the parchment of my heart.

Asking Why

Does there have to be a reason?
Do you ask why the lion ate the lamb?
It needed no reason other than that it was hungry
Perhaps the most evolved trait of humanity
Is not its reason, but the food it has learned to digest
For survival.

Did I Have It Coming?

If Karma measures time
Not by the sun, nor the moon
Neither the seasons, nor the years
Did I sheath a knife in your back
In another life?
Can I make sense of all this:
That your soul remembered my eyes
From a world beyond?

The World I Live In

Machivelli answered a Question
of How
    If the Means
   by which one becomes a Ruler
    and keeps his Power
    Effectively and Efficiently
  are Disturbing to one's Sensibilities
  The Question We Then Ought to Ask is:
    Why do We Wish to Rule
     to Begin With

The Question of Whether Ruling is a Good
Is Not a Question Machiavelli Sought to Answer
Machiavellian is Only an Insult
If you Assume, Presume, that Incompetence
Shall Insulate You from Blame
That it is better to be an inept, stupid ruler
Than a calculated and educated one

In the world I live in,
self-serving incompetence tastes as bitter
as malice.
The customary dose of false sweeteners
fail in their charm,
have me convulsing in dry heaves.

The great malfeasance that soothes the
morally unremarkable:
    I'm not malicious like that
necessitates a degree of proficiency and grit
they don't have
to apply to either good or evil
thus they are more amoral than Machiavelli
without being themselves Machiavellian

You Knew We Were Dead Before I Did

I had to let you bury us
I was suffocating on the soil
Trying to keep it off
Our decaying friendship

In a Court of Narcissism

Everything you say and do
Can and will be held against you
But in the court of dysfunction
Narcissism, presiding
The rules of evidence are volatile
Applied without equity
The jury of flying monkeys
Will receive instructions
Guaranteeing your conviction
And any attempt to mitigate
Your final sentence
Will only secure the maximum

The Forest

I wandered into the forest and its welcome
Was the slowest of quick sands
The transition, significant yet subtle
From slightly encumbered to sufficiently engulfed
Still, the Universe sprinkled breadcrumbs
To truths I was not yet ready to find

A house I found in its depths, appearance inviting
The couple in their apparent solitude
Their reflection could not see
I let them bare their fangs and feed
Preferring to be craved by what consumed

But a monster like me bites back
I bled them while they slept
So when they made a corpse of me
After they were done
I rose stronger than before

When I looked again to the forest

With more curiosity than fear, this time
I found the trail of breadcrumbs
The Universe left for me
And the forest welcomed me home

Nature's Duality

I walk through a forest
and the forest walks through me.
Its wind in my lungs,
my breath in its leaves.
Both blooming with life
as we dance with decay.

Papered Heart

I patched my heart up
With ink and paper so well
I think I might have forgiven you
Still, the time and work it took
Is a constant reminder
To not give it back to you

A Witch's Prayer

As the wheel of fortune turns
So the work of Karma churns
I've found my reprieve
This no more will I grieve
I release the chafe of rage
No more am I bound by its cage
In faith, I embrace this timeline
Peace and prosperity are mine

Milton Keynes UK
Ingram Content Group UK Ltd.
UKHW020951010424
440421UK00016B/1011